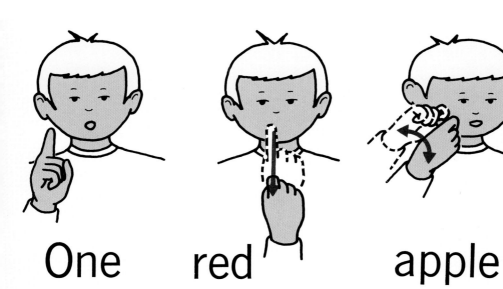

One   red   apple   1

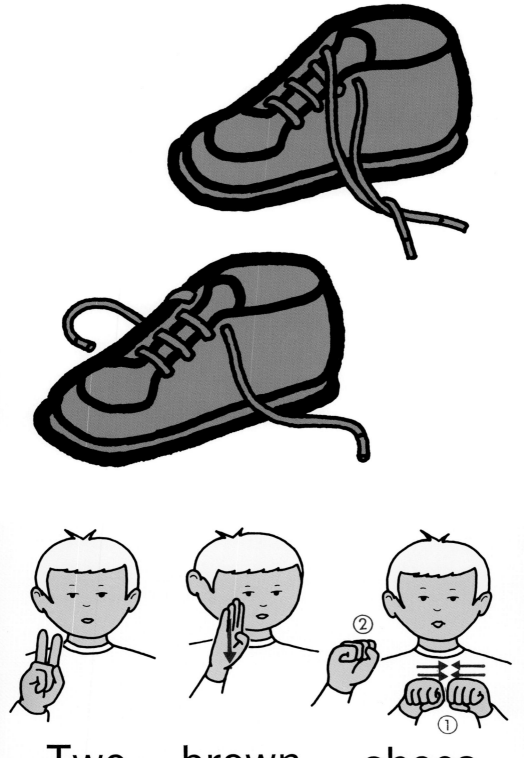

2 Two   brown   shoes

Three yellow umbrellas 3

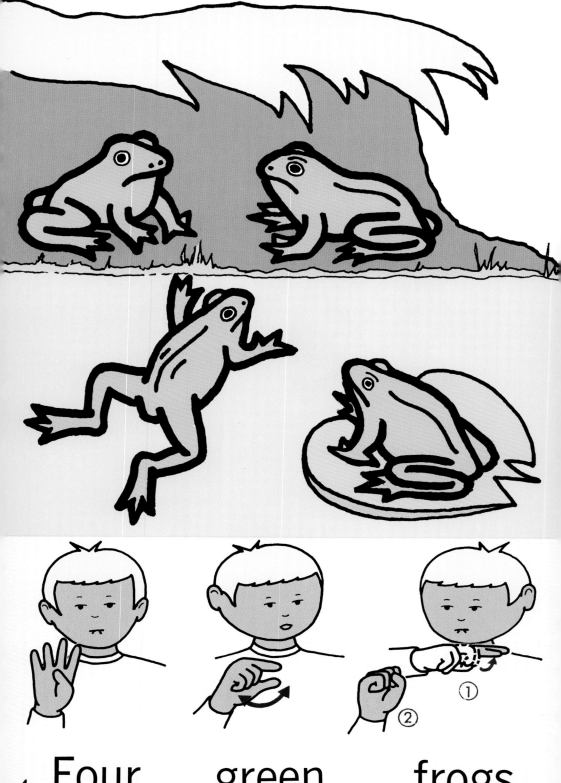

4 Four green frogs

Five grey squirrels

Six   orange

pumpkins

8 Seven   purple   flowers

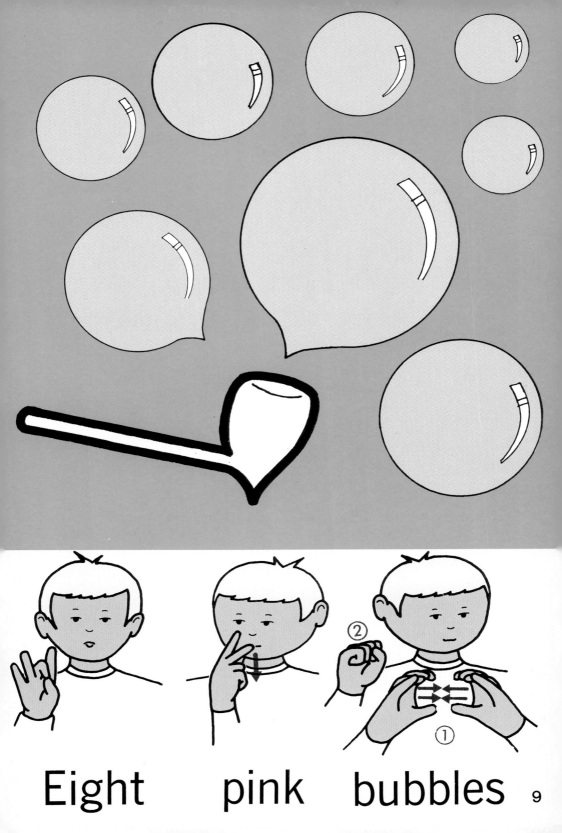

Eight   pink   bubbles 9

Nine   blue

cars

Ten

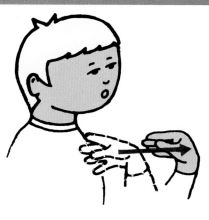 

white   mice

1 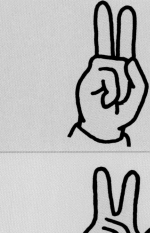 one

2 two

3 three

4 four

5 five

6		six
7		seven
8		eight
9		nine
10		ten

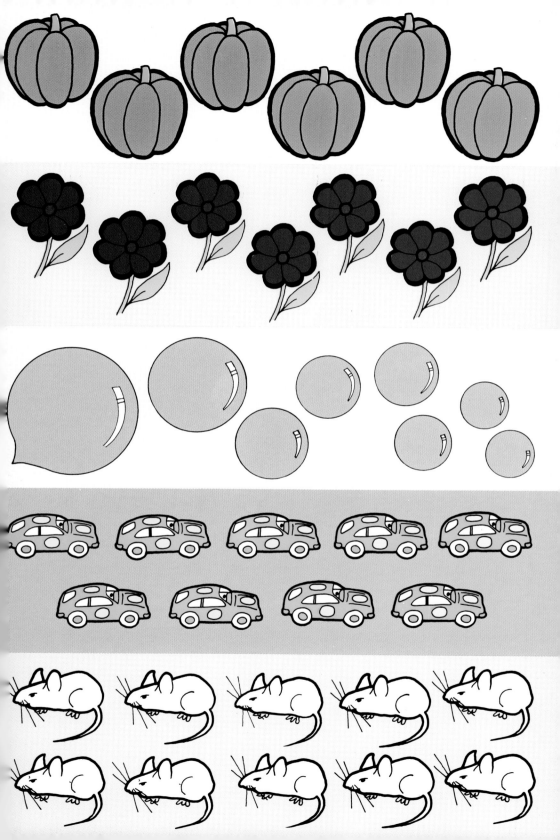

Black

Ask your child—

What's that?

How many —?

What color —?

A
book
about
me

signed
ENGLISH

Prepared under the supervision of the staff of the
Gallaudet Signed English Project:

Text Karen Luczak Saulnier
Lillian B. Hamilton
Howard L. Roy, Consultant
Harry Bornstein, Director
Illustrations Ralph R. Miller, Sr.

This Level I book is about a little girl. It gives the sign words for her family, house, furniture, yard, toys, room, food, and animals. Use the signs when reading the book to your child, and let the child see your lips as you read and sign. This will help your child learn to associate the signs with sounds and lip shapes.

If you have difficulty with any of the signs, consult **The Comprehensive Signed English Dictionary**. In the dictionary, the major reference book of the Signed English series, you will find a large and clear drawing of each sign and a complete word description of how it is formed. In addition, the dictionary explains the nature and use of the Signed English System, a tool designed to aid language development. It is hoped that this book will make the task of learning language more pleasant and improve communication between you and your child.

For more information about other Signed English materials, contact:

Gallaudet University Press
800 Florida Avenue NE
Washington, DC 20002

The Signed English Series

KENDALL GREEN PUBLICATIONS
Gallaudet University Press
Washington, D.C.